DINOS...
OF THE LOWER CRETACEOUS

DAVID & OLIVER WEST

FIREFLY BOOKS

A FIREFLY BOOK

Published by Firefly Books Ltd. 2016

First printing

Publisher Cataloging-in-Publication Data (U.S.)

Names: West, David, 1956-, author.
Title: Dinosaurs of the Lower Cretaceous : 25 dinosaurs / David West.
Description: Richmond Hill, Ontario, Canada : Firefly Books, 2016. | Series: Dinosaurs. | Includes
   index. | Summary: "An illustrated guide of 25 of the best-known dinosaurs of the period,
   providing up-to-date information with highly detailed computer generated artwork. Illustrated
   introductory spreads provide background information on the time periods in which the
   dinosaurs lived" -- Provided by publisher.
Identifiers: ISBN 978-1-77085-831-2 (paperback) | 978-1-77085-832-9 (hardcover)
Subjects: LCSH: Dinosaurs – Juvenile literature.
Classification: LCC QE861.5W478 |DDC 567.9 – dc23

Library and Archives Canada Cataloguing in Publication

West, David, 1956-, author
       Dinosaurs of the lower Cretaceous : 25 dinos... / David West. (Dinosaurs)
Includes index.
ISBN 978-1-77085-832-9 (hardback).--ISBN 978-1-77085-831-2 (paperback)
       1. Dinosaurs--Juvenile literature. 2. Paleontology--Cretaceous--
Juvenile literature. I. Title.
QE861.5.W469 2016   j567.9   C2016-902142-4

Published in the United States by
Firefly Books (U.S.) Inc.
P.O. Box 1338, Ellicott Station
Buffalo, New York 14205

Published in Canada by
Firefly Books Ltd.
50 Staples Avenue, Unit 1
Richmond Hill, Ontario L4B 0A7

Printed in China

Text by David and Oliver West
Illustrations by David West

Produced by David West
Children's Books,
6 Princeton Court, 55 Felsham
Road, London SW15 1AZ

CONTENTS

THE LOWER CRETACEOUS

During the Lower Cretaceous period, 144–127 million years ago, the two landmasses of Laurasia and Gondwana began to break up. The continents we know today became more obvious as they split apart from one another. Temperatures on land and sea were generally warm, but it was much cooler at the poles.

Life in the warm seas continued with the top predators, marine crocodiles, thriving. Nearly all the dinosaur groups of the Upper Jurassic were still around in the Lower Cretaceous period. Most of the large **sauropods** became smaller, although there were one or two exceptions. **Stegosaurs** became less common and then died out, but **ankylosaur** types began to increase. Also appearing in many forms and sizes were dinosaurs with feathers. Evolving alongside were the early birds. Mammals were still small. Flowering plants also began to evolve during this period, and with them, insects and bugs.

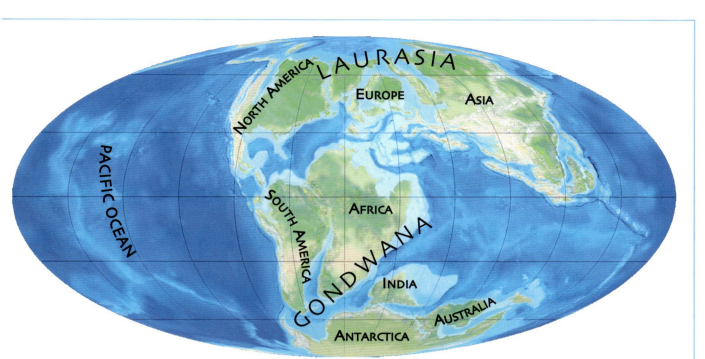

This map shows the Earth at the time of the Cretaceous period 120 million years ago. Below, a scene from the European Cretaceous 130 million years ago shows a Concavenator (1) attacking a Polacanthus (2). In the foreground a group of Pelecanimimuses (3) and Hypsilophodons (4) run for their lives.

AMARGASAURUS

Amargasaurus means "lizard from Amarga," named after the valley in Argentina where its fossils were found. This strange-looking **sauropod** had tall bones rising from its neck and back that might have given it a double, humped-back appearance. It had a long, tapering tail like *Diplodocus* that could be used like a whip in defense against predators.

Amargasaurus lived **132–127 million years ago**. Fossil remains have been found in Argentina, South America. It grew up to 39 feet (12 m) long and weighed around 5.5 tons (5 tonnes).

ARAGOSAURUS

Aragosaurus was named after where it was found in Aragon, Spain. It was a large **sauropod**, very similar to the *Camarasaurus*, which was found in the United States. It had a long neck and tail, a broad body and a compact skull with chisel-like teeth for chomping the vegetation off tall conifer trees.

Aragosaurus lived between **140–121 million years ago**. Its fossil remains were found in Spain, Europe. It grew up to 59 feet (18 m) long and weighed around 30.8 tons (28 tonnes).

BARYONYX

Baryonyx, literally meaning "heavy claw," was first discovered in England, Europe. It was named after the large claw on its first finger, which was 12 inches (31 cm) long. These claws, along with its elongated crocodile-like jaws, suggest that *Baryonyx* hunted mostly fish and scavenged from other sources. This is backed up by the evidence of fossilized remains of a prehistoric fish and flesh from an *Iguanodon* that were found in the stomach of a young *Baryonyx*.

Baryonyx lived **130–125 million years ago**. Fossil remains were found in England and Spain, Europe; and, possibly, North Africa, Africa. It grew to 24.6 feet (7.5 m) in length and weighed 1.3 tons (1.2 tonnes).

BEIPIAOSAURUS

Beipiaosaurus was a feathered **theropod** dinosaur belonging to the **therizinosaur** family. It is named after the Beipiao province in China, Asia, where its fossils were found. It is thought that *Beipiaosaurus* was a herbivore. Its feathers were not for flight but probably for keeping it warm. Longer feathers may have been used in courtship displays.

Beipiaosaurus lived around **127 million years ago**. Fossil remains have only been found in China, Asia. It grew up to 7.2 feet (2.2 m) long and weighed about 187 pounds (85 kg).

CAUDIPTERYX

Caudipteryx, which means "tail feather," was a peacock-sized, feathered **theropod** and a member of the **oviraptors**. It had feathers up to 8 inches (20 cm) long, arranged as a fan at the end of its tail, as well as on its arms. Its body was covered in shorter, downy feathers. Scientists think *Caudipteryx* could have been brightly colored, like modern birds today. Unlike modern birds, though, it would not have been able to fly.

Caudipteryx lived around **124 million years ago**. Fossil remains have only been found in China, Asia. It was a small dinosaur that grew up to 3.3 feet (1 m) long and weighed about 22 pounds (10 kg).

This "humped-back hunter" was a medium-sized, meat-eating **theropod** with some strange characteristics. As its name suggests, it had a hump in the middle of its back that formed a crest. The function of this crest is unknown, but it might have been used as a visual display like the head crests on other dinosaurs. Impressions of the dinosaur's skin showed scales similar to those on an alligator.

Concavenator lived around **130 million years ago**. Fossil remains have been found in Spain, Europe. It grew up to 20 feet (6 m) long and weighed around 2.2 to 3.3 tons (2–3 tonnes).

DILONG

Dilong was a primitive **tyrannosaur** directly related to the famous *Tyrannosaurus rex*. Its name literally means "emperor dragon." Its fossil remains left imprints of feathers so it is thought that its body was covered in feathers. These were probably for insulation rather than flight. The presence of protofeathers shows that *Dilong* might have been warm-blooded, which means it would have been an active hunter. *Dilong* had slightly longer forelimbs than other **tyrannosaurs** and had three fingers on each hand.

Dilong lived **128 million years ago**. Fossil remains have been found in the Liaoning province in China, Asia. It is estimated to have grown up to 6.6 feet (2 m) long and weighed 25 pounds (11.3 kg).

ECHINODON

Echinodon, meaning "hedgehog tooth," was so named because of the spines on its teeth. It was a small, omnivorous dinosaur and a member of the **heterodontosaurs**. It had canine teeth in the front of its beaked mouth, which could have been used for killing small animals. These teeth might also have been used to dig up the roots of plants for a meal that other dinosaurs could not get to.

Echinodon lived **140 million years ago**. Fossil remains have been found in England, Europe. It grew up to 2 feet (60 cm) long and weighed around 5 to 10 pounds (2.2–4.5 kg).

EOTYRANNUS

Eotyrannus was a smaller **tyrannosaur**, with long arms and a slightly elongated neck. It had some of the longest hands amongst non-avian **theropods**, which could have helped it to catch fish and smaller prey. The name *Eotyrannus* means "dawn tyrant." Like other **tyrannosaurs** it had serrated teeth like a steak knife, which could slice through flesh.

Eotyrannus lived **127 million years ago**. Fossil remains were found on the Isle of Wight in England, Europe. It could grow to more than 14 feet (4.3 m) long and weighed in excess of 300 to 500 pounds (136–227 kg).

Fukuiraptor was a small **theropod** found on the island of Japan, Asia, and named after the area where it was found, "Fukui." Although called a raptor, because the large claws on its hands were wrongly identified as the sickle claws of the raptors, it is more likely that *Fukuiraptor* was an **allosaur** or **tyrannosaur**. It was quite small for an **allosaur**, due to island dwarfism. This can happen when a small island habitat does not have enough food resources for an animal to grow larger.

Fukuiraptor lived about **130 million years ago**. Fossil remains have been found in Japan, Asia. It grew up to 14 feet (4.3 m) long and weighed around 450 pounds (204 kg).

HARPYMIMUS

Harpymimus, named after the creature from Greek mythology, means "harpy mimic." It is a **theropod** dinosaur of the **ornithomimosaur** family and was probably omnivorous. The long skull ended in a beak with 11 cylindrical teeth in the lower jaw. These would have been used for gripping small prey or for pulling at parts of plants. It also had long arms and legs, and a long neck. It was extremely agile and speedy, which were skills it needed in order to escape predators.

Harpymimus lived about **130–125 million years ago**. Fossil remains have been found in Mongolia, Asia. It grew to between 6.6 and 9.8 feet (2–3 m) long and is estimated to have weighed up to 110 pounds (50 kg).

Hypsilophodon means "high-ridge tooth." It was a small, plant-eating dinosaur of the bird-hipped order called **ornithischia**. It ran on two legs and was quite fast. It had a beak for cropping vegetation, and teeth at the back of its mouth for chewing. These little dinosaurs probably lived in large groups and are often referred to as the "deer of the Mesozoic."

Hypsilophodon lived around **130–125 million years ago**. Fossil remains have been found in England and Spain, Europe. It grew up to 5.9 feet (1.8 m) long and weighed around 44 pounds (20 kg).

IGUANODON

Iguanodon, meaning "iguana tooth," was a plant-eating **ornithopod** dinosaur that could stand on its two back feet. When traveling, though, it would walk on all fours. It had a beak for biting through tough plants, and teeth to grind the plants into mush before swallowing. Its hands had a little finger that could grasp, and a thumbspike that might have been used as a defensive weapon against predators.

Iguanodon lived **140–110 million years ago**. Fossils have been found in England, Germany, Spain and Belgium, Europe; and the United States, North America. It grew to 33 feet (10 m) long and weighed 3.3 tons (3 tonnes).

KINNAREEMIMUS

Kinnareemimus was a small **theropod** dinosaur of the **ornithomimosaur** family. It was named in honor of Kinnaree, a mythical being from Thai mythology with the body of a woman and the legs of a bird. Its fossilized foot bones suggest it was adapted for swift running, and like most **ornithomimosaurs**, it was probably an omnivore.

Kinnareemimus lived around **139–112 million years ago**. Fossil remains have been found in Thailand, Asia. It grew up to 9.9 feet (3 m) long and weighed around 175 pounds (79.3 kg).

MANTELLISAURUS

Mantellisaurus was similar to Iguanodon (see page 18) but with a lighter build and shorter forelimbs. It was an **ornithopod** that was probably bipedal and only went on all fours when it traveled. It is named after its discoverer, Gideon Mantell, an English paleontologist.

Mantellisaurus lived around **135–125 million years ago**. Fossil remains have been found in England, Europe. It grew up to 23 feet (7 m) long and weighed around 0.75 tons (0.68 tonnes).

MEI

Mei was a small, duck-sized **troodon** dinosaur. *Mei* means "sleeping" in Chinese, and it was so-called because the fossil was in a sleeping position with its snout nestled beneath one of the forelimbs. It was preserved when it was suddenly covered in volcanic ash as it slept. It had many sharp, serrated teeth, keen senses and stereoscopic vision. It had sickle claws and raptor-like hands. It was probably omnivorous, but would have chosen to eat rodents, dinosaur hatchlings or possibly even stolen eggs!

Mei lived approximately **130 million years ago**. Fossil remains were found in found in the Liaoning province in China, Asia. The juvenile fossil found was about 21 inches (53 cm) long and weighed 0.8 to 1.87 pounds (0.36–0.85 kg).

NEOVENATOR

Neovenator is one of the best-known of the large carnivorous dinosaurs found in Western Europe. Its name means "new hunter." It was a lightweight, agile **allosaur theropod**. It had powerful back legs that allowed it to run down prey quickly. It had grasping hands and a mouth full of blade-like teeth. It probably preyed on *Iguanodons* (see page 18).

Neovenator lived about **127 million years ago**. Fossil remains were found on the Isle of Wight in England, Europe. It is thought they could grow to 33 feet (10 m) long and weigh up to 2.2 tons (2 tonnes).

Pelecanimimus means "pelican mimic," which refers to its long snout and throat pouch, similar to those on pelicans. It was a small **ornithomimosaur** with about 220 very small teeth. It might have used these to catch fish and small animals. It had long arms with clawed, grasping hands. It lived alongside *Concavenator* (see page 11), which may have preyed on it.

Pelecanimimus lived around **130 million years ago**. Fossil remains have been found in Spain, Europe. It grew up to 7 feet (2.1 m) long and could weigh up to 100 pounds (45 kg).

PELOROSAURUS

Pelorosaurus, which means "monstrous lizard," was the first-ever named **sauropod**. Originally believed to be a large aquatic crocodile, it was reclassified as a dinosaur and named *Pelorosaurus* in 1850. It was a very large, quadrupedal herbivore, similar to *Brachiosaurus*, with a very long neck and substantial mass! It lived in the wooded areas of Western Europe where its long neck allowed it to feed on the topmost branches of conifers.

Pelorosaurus lived between **140–125 million years ago**. Its fossils have been found in England and possibly Portugal, Europe. It was between 52.5 and 82 feet (16–25 m) long and weighed 16.5 to 22 tons (15–20 tonnes.)

Polacanthus was an **ankylosaur**, a quadrupedal herbivore with thick protective armor and spikes. It had short legs, and it used its beak to crop low-lying plants. Its name means "many thorns." Above the hips it had a large shield of bone that protected it from the jaws of large predators. The rest of its armor on the tail, shoulders and neck was covered in spikes. It even had armored eyelids.

Polacanthus lived approximately **130–125 million years ago**. Its fossil remains were found on the Isle of Wight in England, Europe. It grew up to 16 feet (5 m) long and could weigh up to 2.2 tons (2 tonnes).

Shamosaurus was a medium-sized **ankylosaur**. Its name means "desert sand reptile." Thick, leathery skin covered in bony nodules and sharp spikes running down its flanks gave this dinosaur plenty of protection. It also had a club on the end of its tail that it would swing to defend itself from meat-eating predators.

Shamosaurus lived around **127 million years ago**. Fossil remains have been found in Mongolia, Asia. It grew up to 16.4 feet (5 m) long and weighed around 2 tons (1.8 tonnes).

Siamotyrannus means "Siamese tyrant," and was named after the old Thai kingdom of Siam. *Siamotyrannus* was a carnivorous **theropod** dinosaur. It might have hunted dinosaurs such as the **ornithomimosaur** *Kinnareemimus* (see page 19), and the large **titanosaur** *Phuwiangosaurus*.

Siamotyrannus lived **135 million years ago**. Fossil remains have been found in Thailand, Asia. It grew up to 19.6 feet (6 m) long and weighed around 0.5 tons (0.45 tonnes).

SINOSAUROPTERYX

Sinosauropteryx means "Chinese dragon wing." *Sinosauropteryx* was a small, lightweight predator, hunting small lizards and mammals. It was the first **theropod** dinosaur to be found with protofeathers. These feathers kept it warm. One of the fossils found was so well-preserved that there were two eggs in its abdomen, ready to be laid, and the contents of its stomach included small lizards and mammals.

Sinosauropteryx lived **135–121 million years ago**. Fossil remains have been found in the Liaoning province in China, Asia. It grew up to lengths of just over 3.3 feet (1 m) and weighed up to 1.2 pounds (0.5 kg).

VALDOSAURUS

Valdosaurus was a fast-moving, bipedal herbivore. Its name means "Weald lizard," which is the name of the area where it was discovered in southwest England, Europe. It was an **ornithopod** whose fantastic jaws and digestive system were perfect for breaking down the harsh plant material it fed on.

Valdosaurus lived **142–121 million years ago**. Its fossil remains were found in south England and Romania, Europe, and Niger, Africa. It may have grown to 14.4 feet (4.4 m) long and weighed around 110 pounds (50 kg).

Wuerhosaurus was a **stegosaur** dinosaur. Its name comes from the city of Wuerho where it was found in China, Asia. Like other **stegosaurs**, it had bony plates along its back that may have helped regulate its body temperature. It also had a set of spikes, called a thagomizer, at the end of its tail. It would have used this to defend itself against predators. It had shorter legs than *Stegosaurus*, which allowed it to feed on plants closer to the ground.

Wuerhosaurus lived around **139–132 million years ago**. Fossil remains have been found in China and Mongolia, Asia. It grew to an estimated 23 feet (7 m) long and weighed around 1.1 tons (1 tonne).

allosaur
A member of a group of large, bipedal, carnivorous dinosaurs, common in North America.

ankylosaur
A family of bulky, quadrupedal, armored dinosaurs that had a club-like tail. The family included *Ankylosaurus* and *Euoplocephalus*.

heterodontosaur
A member of the family of "bird-hipped" dinosaurs, believed to be primitive ornithopods.

ornithischia
A group of dinosaurs characterized by their "bird-hips" and beaks.

ornithomimosaur
A family of theropod dinosaurs that looked like modern ostriches, which included *Pelecanimimus*, *Gallimimus* and *Deinocheirus*.

ornithopod
A group of bird-hipped dinosaurs characterized by being fast-paced grazers, becoming one of the most successful herbivore groups.

oviraptor
A family of bird-like, omnivorous dinosaurs with toothless, parrot-like beaks and bony crests. The family included *Citipati* and *Gigantoraptor*.

sauropod
A group of large, four-legged, herbivorous dinosaurs with long necks and long tails. This group included the well-known *Brachiosaurus*, *Diplodocus* and *Apatosaurus*.

stegosaur
A member of a group of quadrupedal herbivores, characterized by their bony plates and, occasionally, a thagomizer.

therizinosaur
A member of a group of giant-clawed theropods.

theropod
The large group of lizard-hipped dinosaurs that walked on two legs and included most of the giant carnivores such as *Tyrannosaurus*.

titanosaur
A family of sauropod dinosaurs that included some of the heaviest animals ever to walk the Earth such as *Argentinosaurus*.

troodon
A group of bird-like theropod dinosaurs.

tyrannosaur
A family of carnivorous theropod dinosaurs that included the famous Tyrannosaurus rex.

INDEX